sand & water

Clifton King

sand & water

First Edition

ISBN 978-0-9786935-4-1

Library of Congress Control Number: 2018908013

Cover photo by the author:
low tide at Ponto Beach, Carlsbad, California

Printed in the United States of America

Royale Road Publishing

for Katie Rose, my family & friends & for you

I am the poet of the body,
and the poet of the soul.

Walt Whitman

Author's note

This is a collection of old & new poems with a few random thoughts thrown in. The majority of these poems have never seen the printed page. A few were published in slightly different versions in: *Summation, San Diego Poetry Annual, poetry organic, Magee Park Poets Anthology* and *Beachcombing.* But for most, this is their first outing. Many were rescued from the dusty drawers of an old desk; others, gleaned from the hard drive of an ancient Windows 98 computer I discovered while cleaning out the hall closet. Several were found between the pages of various poetry books, no doubt placed there as I struggled with literary ethics & my desire to steal some of the better lines. While I did not intend this collection to have a theme, the Pacific Ocean has surfaced as the main character, with love, both found & lost, in a supporting role & death lurking in the background like an extra trying to get his face on camera.

Poems are in no special order, with two exceptions.

Hostage Situation is on page 6, the date in April, 2018 when the "Zero Tolerance Policy" was implemented with Gestapo-like forced separation of immigrant children from their parents.

Fourteen Empty Desks is on page 17,
the number of innocent students & teachers murdered in Parkland.

Clifton King
July, 2018

Contents

At the touch of love
everyone becomes a poet.

Plato

Pagan Burial

I'm afraid that when I die
my poetry book collection
will be boxed up, donated
to the library bookstore,
sold for pennies on the dollar.
And those unfinished poems
scattered about my desk,
waiting on just the right words
to complete them, will become
fodder for the recycle bin.
I can't slip my favorites
into a pocket, take them with me.
How can God ask me to never
indulge in another poem, or pen
not even a couplet, ever again?
I cannot live with that scenario,
do not want to die believing it.
So, here are my final instructions:
lay me out in the bottom
of an old wooden boat; pile
poetry books, my desk debris,
over and around that cold
nothingness I will have become;
sprinkle with 90 proof Bacardi,
set ablaze, launch me toward
the setting sun. Better a pagan burial
than eternity without poetry.

Beach Girl

I stop at my favorite café, order coffee,
wander out to a sidewalk table
next to a group of old surfers, guys
with skin like leather from all those years
on the water, guys wearing shorts,
sweatshirts, flip flops just as they have
for decades. I settle in with a book
I can't seem to get into. They talk about
swell direction, argue whether Swami's
or Trestles has the best right. They laugh
about John's old truck that threw a rod
on the way to Wind 'n Sea, complain about
the parking meters in Oceanside.
I sense a change in the chatter, peek over
my reading glasses, see a twenty-something
woman at their table. Long sun-bleached
hair falls down her smooth back, skin
luminescent with youth. This is the same
beach girl look I couldn't resist
when we first met. Your blond curls
trying to escape from under that sunhat,
the color of summer painted on your face.
And I knew I wanted to spent the rest of my life
under the influence of your sea-blue eyes.

California Gray

What has drawn her into the channel
at Agua Hedionda lagoon?
Her barnacled body struggles,
rolls on its side, flipper exposed
at an odd angle, like the sail
of a boat adrift on a stormy sea.
She labors to recover & surface
for a breath. Every wave disrupts
her progress. There is no power
in the sweep of her mighty tail.
People crowd the jetties,
line the highway bridge.
A hundred iphones capture
the moment. Three girls
joke as they try for a selfie,
whale in the background.
Children, atop their fathers' shoulders,
laugh & shout in that shrill voice
of youth. A guy, on his phone,
explains to his girlfriend why he'll be late.
The Gray slips under the highway bridge.
The outflow carries her back
down the channel toward the sea.
She begins her struggle anew,
rolls onto her side & sinks.
Her long, slender shape
a dark scar on the white sand bottom.
But, the crowd has lost interest.
Only a few remain to witness the end.
There is nothing to be done,
like the morning my mother died
—within reach, but beyond help.

Father, I Thought I Saw You

I thought I saw you downtown
in that little cafe where we ate lunch
most days. You were at our favorite table
in the back, near the window,
where we would watch the sidewalk
show of tourists and locals.
Yesterday you were in the yard,
in that corner where crows congregate
every morning near that old rose bush
with its scarlet blossoms.
But it was only a whisper of leaves
whipped by the wind, silent in its chaos.
I thought I saw you today at the beach
down along water's edge. You know,
that stretch of shore where I waded in,
let your ashes drift out with the tide
that August day all those years ago.
I thought I saw you today.
But, it was just a flash of light
off the ocean, a breaking wave,
the confusion of sea and sunlight.

December 22, 2017
Ponto Jetties

The air is December cold,
the sea, slate gray.
A small swell sweeps down
from the northwest.
Morning sun shimmers
on the face of each wave
before it spills over onto itself.
Two days from now will mark
the beginning of my seventy-fifth year,
decades of flirting with the tides,
the many moods of an uncertain sea.
I wander out onto the granite architecture
that is the north jetty, amazed
that man still believes he can control
the ocean, dictate her behavior.
Seagulls feast on mussels exposed
by a low tide. That vast expanse
of beach created by a retreating sea
will disappear in a matter of hours
as the tide turns. I consider paddling out,
allow the sea to consume me.
In her embrace I am a young man,
the world, anything I can imagine.

Hostage Situation

A terrorist
has taken two thousand children
hostage,
two thousand children
ripped from their mothers' arms,
hauled away like so much livestock,
interned in chain link cages,
all in the name of national security.
The terrorist says
small children are a very real threat,
especially the brown ones.
The terrorist wants a wall
in exchange
for the return of brown children,
in exchange
for reuniting families,
brown families, brown families
he doesn't want in this country.
The terrorist
justifies his inhumane acts
with ill-informed babble.
It's the law, he claims.
Not a trace of human decency
can be gleaned
from his incoherent blather,
not a speck of empathy.
These children cry for their mothers.
Mothers cry for their babies.
The American Terrorist goes golfing.

Winter

I'm not sure when winter begins
since I live in a California summer.

I'm not sure I'd recognize the season:
sullen skies suspended outside my window,
a chill that marches straight to the bone.

I'm not sure if that's winter—or old age.
I'm not sure there's a difference.

Waiting Blossoms

Afternoon clouds fall
into Monet's lily pond,
float on mirrored waters
among blossoms that wait
for brush and pigment
to harvest them.

But, there is no palette of oils,
no flourish of brush strokes.
And that painter, who imagined
what others could not, rests
in a garden behind the church
in Giverny. Forever home.

Memphis Mayor's Message
to Striking Sanitation Workers, 1968
Inspired by Patrick Brown's painting *I am a Man (Memphis 1968)*

Martin Luther King Jr. said of this strike, on March 18, 1968:
We've got to give ourselves to this struggle until the end.
Martin Luther King Jr. was assassinated in Memphis on April 4, 1968.

your faces are black
we do not acknowledge you
wave your signs
sing and march arm in arm
we will not acknowledge you
we will not spend money
to better job safety for black men
we do not care
about black men crushed to death
by a trash truck
we do not care about wages
so low you must rely on food stamps
to feed your families
we will not listen to your demands
as you march peacefully to city hall
instead we will mace you
tear gas you
bring out dogs and night sticks
we will call up the national guard
put tanks in the streets
but we will not spend money
on job safety and better wages
for black men
we do not care
we will not acknowledge you
we do not see you as human beings

Tuesday at the Marina

Boats line up along B dock,
yacht club in the background
with its *members only* bar.
There, Captain Karl, senior sailor
in the marina, regales others
with his mighty mariner tales.
That's Karl's small sloop
huddled between that thirty footer
with the brown sail cover
and the old wooden power boat
with those green gunwales.
A school teacher from Escondido
owns the thirty footer.
She comes over weekends,
shares her forward berth
with a young man from the power boat.
But, today is Tuesday. Not a breath
of wind to texture the water,
no slap of halyards, not a sail raised.
The boats rest on their reflections,
wait for wind, wait for the weekend.

Window Box

A murder of crows swarms a eucalyptus out back.
The sky is dark with black feathered forms,
their raucous conversation sunup to sundown.
Out front our window box is alive with geranium
blossoms, red as a California coastal sunset;
leaves, green as a winter sea.
We water it with an old galvanized
watering can filled from a rain barrel
that sits beneath a downspout.
A pair of house finches pick through
the mass of vegetation, scavenging
for nest building material. The male
displays that red breast of spring,
the female dressed in the drab brown
feathers she will wear year-round.
They sing as they work. A song similar
to the common canary. The female
plucks and pulls, the male stands guard.
Across the street, perched in a palm tree,
a lone crow watches. The finches fly off
with their harvest. This may be the same pair
that nested under our porch eaves last year,
eggs sheltered from the hot sun,
inclement weather—but not the crows.

Contemplating the Day

I am content here,
morning sun warm
on my face,
no intentions for the day
other than
a few cups of coffee
and a walk on the beach
where I might find
answers to questions
that have followed me
throughout my life.

Cell Phone Lot
San Diego Airport

It's like an ant colony,
a constant string of cars
coming and going.
They stay just long enough
to get that call, then leave
to pick up someone,
take them somewhere.
From where I'm parked
I can't determine
who that someone is, where
that somewhere might be.
My phone rings.
I know this someone,
I know the locale of somewhere.
Two out of three isn't bad.
I've been here more than an hour,
arrived right on time for
the twelve-ten flight from Seattle.
But, she was on the one-ten flight
—just as planned.
This did however,
give me time to write this poem.

Local Girl
—for Janine

She's a local girl,
keeps the summer sun
in her pocket.
I love the sun, she says,
wearing its glow
on her face,
a tan harvested
from the sun's smile.
I love the sun, she says,
her heart
warm with sunlight,
a gift
to every person she meets.
She's a local girl.
How lucky for us.

Letter from God

Yesterday I received a letter from God,
not one of those mental images that rattles around in your head
like a single pea in a pod, nor did it cause me to speak in tongues
or burst into flames, it was an *honest-to-God* letter printed
on scenic stationary, the Sea of Galilee I believe, yet,
there was no return address, though the *forever* stamp
was cancelled in San Diego, a fact the Chamber of Commerce
could capitalize on, *San Diego, home of the Padres and God,*
but the idea that God uses the US Postal Service
to spread His message scares the hell out of me,
so I saved the letter, slipped it into my Bible,
& while we're on the subject I just can't get into Bible stories,
take Adam & Eve, he sends her to the marketplace for fruit,
specifically asks for pears but Eve brings back an apple,
tells Adam the produce guy said one bite could change their lives,
get them out of that rut they're in, eat, sleep, eat, sleep,
lie around naked, & we're supposed to believe all mankind
has since been cursed, burdened with daily chores, weeds
in the garden, a mortgage, a spouse that won't shut up,
& the certainty of death because Eve picked a round fruit
instead of one shaped like J.Lo, & then there's the Ark,
centuries of human unrest, debauchery & toga parties
so God decides to wipe us out, but save the animals,
even the serpents, go figure, & Noah & Sons
come in with the low bid, begin construction
right there in the front yard, ignore zoning laws & codes,
& what a great idea, put lions & antelope together
in a confined space for forty days & forty nights,
but today PETA protects animals while millions of people
go hungry & homeless, & God promises everlasting life,
that is, if the mail carrier doesn't lose your letter.

Dictionary

I love paging through that book.
There's something about a printed page,

the way your finger flows down the words,
across that smooth surface.

Then, the turn, that delicate flutter of paper
strong enough to survive years of use.

And the words, those beautiful words,
waiting for the poet to arrange them,
                          give them as gifts.

Fourteen Empty Desks
Parkland

Those children sleep now,
that eternal sleep of death.
And let's not forget their teachers.
Seventeen souls given to God.
Teachers and students slaughtered
by the roar of an AR-15,
by a boy possessed, a boy
in possession of a weapon of war
easier to obtain than a driver's license.
Seventeen bodies on the floor.
Fourteen empty desks.
One more meaningless message
from those cowards in Washington:
...prayers and thoughts...
One more meaningless message
but no action from those cowards
afraid of the NRA, afraid of being
called names by tRump on Twitter,
afraid to act, afraid to protect our children
because of what it might cost them.
Cowards all.

Lie

The photograph makes him question his mirror.
Is it being unfaithful, while this snapshot
of him speaks the truth? The eyes seem
the same, even though they now need
reading glasses. But what about
that sun damaged skin, those random
wrinkles, that sag under his chin?
The hair is still blond, just as in his youth.
Of course, there is the gray around the temples.
What is it people say, *distinguished looking*?
He thinks of Sean Connery or Cary Grant
as *distinguished*, not a guy in shorts
and a Hawaiian shirt. But in truth
he doesn't think about his age that much.
Except maybe in the morning when he
tosses back the covers and sits on the edge
of the bed. There's that little twinge
in his back; that distant ache in his ankle,
broken twice racing motorcycles at an age
when he should have been playing golf.
He steps to the mirror, studies the reflection.
Yes, this is the man he is. That photograph:
a lie, an anomaly of digital imagery.

Sea Breeze

A sea breeze whispers ashore,
leaves the ocean ruffled with whitecaps,

carves beach sand into ridges & valleys,
gives rise to a lazy line of pelicans,

pulls at the subtle curve of palms
that sway & write your name in the sky.

If I could be…

any automobile that has been, or is,
I would be a 1950 Chevrolet sedan.
I would be black in color.
I would be owned by the King family.
In my front seat, Clifton Sr. and Rose Marie,
still in love after ten years of marriage
and those war years that kept them apart.
In my back seat, Clifton Jr., Patricia, Royan,
squabbling over who gets to sit
by the windows, draw pictures
on the glass in the haze of their breath.
I would hear their words, their laughter
and sometimes the sound of tears.
I would carry them to the beach,
to the mountains, surround them
with my stamped steel love.
I would be that automobile,
not for its street prowess or luxury,
but for those years and the chance
to have those memories.

Love Is Not About Numbers

I have lost my sense
of time. Hours,
uncountable as the stars,
have grown into years.
Yet love is not
about numbers:
how many times
it takes our journey
together
to circle the sun,
or how long that trail
of footprints
in the sands
of our history.
We have survived
the tides
of our emotions,
our love still as bright
as a morning sunrise.
And, I want you
for all time
no matter the numbers.

Everest

I am the mountain besieged by climbers
eager to attack my summit; climbers who
linger on my slopes while their fingers
& toes freeze & their noses disappear
from their faces, climbers with ropes
& ice axes & black sunglasses.
They pitch tents & wait while I scowl
& whip up a wind to hide my summit.
They melt ice to make tea, pray
they can learn to breath what isn't here.
Climbers from every corner of earth struggle,
wander lost in my flurries, die a few feet
from their tents or just walk off into the night.
I am the mountain, tired of the hoards that litter
& trample me in the name of conquest. I am tired
of listening to the dead cry out from icy graves.

Command Performance
New Year's Eve

We never know when
the final curtain
will come down,
when we will watch
our last sunset.
Yet, we gather to celebrate
the year to come,
sure that the crimson sky
we watched last night,
darken and disappear,
will take the stage again
in this theater of life.
Encore! Encore!
We wait in the wings
hopeful of answering the call.

Family Portrait

The photograph was taken in the late forties.
My mother's hairstyle speaks as much
to the date as my memory. Even though
it's a black and white, I'm certain her dress
is navy blue with a white collar.
On her finger is a simple gold wedding band.
Her smile says more than the camera
can capture. My father sits close to her.
Their shoulders press against each other.
Just outside the frame of the photograph
he moves his foot next to hers
with a playful tap. His dark, double breasted
suit is the only one he owns. His smile
is genuine but cautious, too many recent
war memories behind those blue eyes.
My younger sister sits on my mother's lap,
leans to the side, tries to see around
the camera, see the photographer.
Mother has an arm around my sister's waist,
a firm grip on her hand. My father holds
my youngest sister cradled in his arm
against his body. Her small hands rest on his.
Not holding on, just staying in touch.
Her gaze is directed at something other than
the camera. I stand next to my mother,
lean in close, hand on her shoulder.
My hair is parted on the left, like my father's.
My shirt is missing a button.
This black and white family portrait
is alive with the colors of hopes and dreams.

Poetry Reading

He wore a fishing vest & faded blue jeans,
a flannel shirt that wouldn't stay tucked
in over his ample belly. He had a quirky
way of looking up at the ceiling every
now & then. Of course he was a poet.
He was the featured poet, a recently
retired English professor & his wife's
third husband. She was there, in the front
row, seemingly to orchestrate the show,
quick to catch his errors & offer comment.
But he seemed content. So on he rambled
about his Jeep & desolate desert roads,
getting lost, stranded at night, the fright
of hanging a wheel off a cliff. Then, almost
as justification for this bold behavior,
he read a plethora of poems about his cancer,
his wife's cancer. He stripped himself naked,
laid body parts on the dais for all to see.
Then I overheard him whisper to her,
I'm tired, let's go home. At that moment
cancer & chemo were more than just words
this poet had woven into his poems. My applause
had been polite, but in my heart I gave that rumpled
old man a standing ovation—just for being there.

Emerging Memories

I remember your eyes,
dark as a moonless night,
warm as an August morning.
I remember your hair,
always a little unruly,
how you peeked out
from that brunette tousle.
I remember that you
smelled like the sky.
I remember the shape
of your lips when you
spoke my name
and that your mouth
tasted like summer.
I remember your touch,
our nights together.
Yet,
I cannot recall why you left.

Chocolate

It would be difficult to compare
women & chocolate.

Sweet, bitter sweet, light, dark
& then there is chocolate.

Should I speak of chocolate,
a mouthful of delight.

Or first indulge in a woman's kiss
to confirm—there is no comparison.

When it is done…

let me slip beneath the sea,
plunge to her depths
                    and rest,
my flesh for the scavengers,
never to be in the earth,
                    bones in a box,
covered over and trampled upon.

Glorious repose,
forever in the thunder of waves.

Last Will & Testament

To my children:

I leave nothing
I take it all with me
I take man's inhumanity to man
I take terrorism, war & men who wage it
I take greed, stupidity, insensitivity
I take politicians, liars, cheats
I take hunger, poverty, illiteracy
I take murder, rape, incest
I take tyranny, bigotry, cruelty
I take cancer, aids, every affliction known
I take what was left to me—with me

gift

I give you the sky
every cloud

every ray of sunlight
that endless blue

the darkness
that cradles stars

the in-between time
of sunrise and sunset

I know you deserve more
but this is all I have to give

stillness

there is the stillness of dawn
  before wildflowers wake
the stillness before we whisper
  I love you the first time
the stillness of a sparrow's stare
  silent in nest
the stillness of a doe in meadow grass
  before she bolts
the stillness before gulls takes flight
  whisper of wings on wind
the stillness of footprints in sand
  waiting on the tide
the stillness before that chaotic collage
  of sunset
then that stillness of eternal sleep
  after mourners weep

Sol

You lay down shadows
long enough to reach

from rooftop to street,
distorted shapes that fall

on flowerbeds still damp
from yesterday's rain.

You sneak through
window shades,

crawl across the carpet
on little cat feet

like Sandburg's fog.
Then you slip from sight,

invite in the night, where
the memory of her still lives.

Havana Revisited

I knew her when I was young
and quick to fall in love.
She was a girl with skin the color
of coffee with a dollop of cream,
eyes dark as burnt toast.
She lived in that old blue house
just beyond that red Ford parked
in a stagnant pool of yesterday's rain.
I remember these filthy gutters,
concrete patchwork sidewalks,
those rusty wrought iron balconies,
the way morning sun streams
down Calle Obispo forcing its way
through the dirty windows
of that small café where we met.
She left one morning without a word,
a young bird who found her wings.

Outside a Poetry Workshop

We meet quite by chance
as she steps into the afternoon,
             leaves the stale air
of memories behind.

We share friendship,
stories of family and lovers,
speak of things that are right,
             others that are not.

             Her thoughts,
blood fresh from her heart,
smear the page.

I read over her shoulder.
Words rise and fall from her lips.

Those soft sounds of her life
mingle with the breeze, lost
among the leaves of a nearby elm.

Osprey

You wing in and alight every evening
just before dark. Why have you chosen
this perch, the yardarm of our flagpole?
Why not the branches of an elm
or sycamore? You roost here all night,
alone, bathed in the same light
as Old Glory. Where is your mate,
your nest. Do you have eggs to tend,
young to raise. Or do you come here
to mourn the loss of nestlings
to an owl or raccoon. You are welcome
to stay in your sorrow. But, we
who watch will continue to rejoice
in the splendor of your feathered form.

raindrops

rain came today
each drop
heavy with heaven

that smell
of freshly washed
souls

the glisten
of innocent eyes

the soft sound
of each drop's
collision with earth

rain came today
then left

as quickly
as she left him

February Whale Watching

The bluff where I stand is scarred
by eons of wind and stormy seas.
The Pacific is dappled with whitecaps.
Above it, an angry sky, threatening clouds.
A north wind bites at my face.
A woman on the beach, her pant legs
rolled up to mid-calf but wet
well above her knees, picks up a shell,
examines it, then tosses it into the sea.
Barefoot, she steps gingerly
on a blanket of beach cobbles,
ropes of kelp rotting along shore.
Her dog, a yellow Lab, runs free,
chases gulls, dashes franticly
in and out of the whitewater.
Two days ago I saw four
California Grays from this bluff.
Their massive backs glistened
in the sun when they surfaced,
spouts hung in the air,
an announcement,
ghost-like against a blue sky.
Today, no shiny arched backs,
not a single blow on the horizon.
Yet, the beauty of sea and sky
is no less. If only you were here.

Ocotillo Sunset

after the art of Patricia Titus:
Ocotillo Sunset

The Sonoran Desert lives on this canvas:
sky ablaze, or has the setting sun
settled amongst branches
of that Desert Coral creating
a conflagration not seen since God
spoke to Moses from a burning bush;
distant mountains, blood red
with evening shadows that spill purple
onto the desert floor; that sparse
green growth struggling to survive
another dusty desert day;
dry riverbeds waiting for a flood of rain
that seldom shows. The desert lives
in the mind's eye of the artist,
in the pigment, in each brush stroke.

Getting the Car Serviced

I pull into the dealer's lot behind a long line
of vehicles. We inch our way toward the bowels
of the Service Department. Customer Care techs
swarm like bees in a field of wildflowers.
A young man approaches. He is *over-the-top* polite,
well groomed, impeccably dressed.
I want to invite him to dinner, introduce him
to my daughter, offer him one of my kidneys
if the need ever arises. Yet, at the same time
I'm *old school,* want a mechanic like those
of my youth. Like Tom Peterson's dad who owned
a Shell station in Norwalk in the fifties and sixties:
oily overalls, grease under his nails, a three day
stubble, a stump of cigar that danced
in the corner of his mouth when he talked.
That single service bay, lined with bright red
tool chests, held the secrets that kept
our *hand-me-down* cars on the road. Out back,
between the station and the Ford dealership,
an old man named Oliver washed cars.
That's the mechanic I want. That's where I want
my car serviced and washed. But now, I give
Polite Guy my keys, wander into the waiting room.
It's not Peterson's Shell station. The coffee bar
offers free Starbucks and pastries. The chairs
are comfortable. The WiFi is working.
It might be time to leave *Old School* in the past.

Venice Beach

Some come to skate or bike
the boardwalk: girls in bikinis
with their slender tan legs;
guys too cool for a shirt,
bodies emblazoned with inked art.
Some come to grunt & sweat
& heft iron in the sand. Thick
necks, rippled abs glisten in the sun.
Some come for beach volleyball
where spikes & full body sacrifices
offer one last chance at fame.
Some come to sit on wooden benches,
watch weirdoes & wait
for the rest of their life to begin.

Library Trip

There on the third shelf,
standing like soldiers at attention,
travel books about Europe.
I pull Paris from the lineup.
A week in Frankfurt leans left,
fills in the gap between
France and Germany.
There is a single book on Spain.
My love never expressed a desire
to visit Madrid or Barcelona.
I leave Spain on the shelf,
take Paris home with me.
I unfold maps, peruse hotel listings,
wonder if making love in France
will be all that different than here,
the Pacific whispering in the background.
Yet, the thought of us sharing coffee
in a Parisian café, strolling
cobblestone paths along the River Seine,
spending Paris nights together
learning the intimate language of touch,
drives me to the airline's website
in search of flight schedules.

Black & White

It shares a shelf with tintypes of people
I may or may not be related to. A black & white
of my mother & father. 1942 is my guess.
She leans into him, both cradled in the crook
of an old elm, rooted deep, clinging to earth
as they all spin through the universe
under God's watchful eye. I can feel that elm's
rough bark, scarred from those heartless
Rhode Island winters; smell wet grass
under foot; taste Autumn in the air;
hear the constant quiet of bare branches.
A photograph is merely a slice of time.
I don't know if that elm survived winters
beyond that one. I do know Mother & Father
flourished through all the seasons of life
& completed their journey—still together.

Colors

Blue is the desert sky after a summer rain,
a mountain lake in the late afternoon;
gold, a Kansas prairie on a summer day,
clouds lingering under a September moon.

Red is the sunrise on a cold, clear morning,
the flight of a hawk overhead on wing;
yellow, a cloudless sunset over the Pacific,
a field of Sunflowers in the spring.

Silver is moonlight on fresh snow,
the wake of a ship under sail;
white, a wave spent, dying along a rocky shore,
the far away spout of a Humpback whale.

Gray is a Dolphin's playful leap from the sea,
green, a saguaro cactus jutting into an Arizona sky,
black, the long shadow of night,
                              the color of eternity.

Innocence

a child
raises her face
to the sky
eyes wrinkled
in a smile
raindrops
tickle her face
play across
her lips
sweet
on her tongue
she laughs
with joy
how precious
the gift of rain
her innocence

What Not to Say
—to win a poetry slam

I went to a poetry slam,
light on poetry—heavy on slam.
But then what can you expect from a concept
conjured up in a Chicago bar?

I went to a poetry slam,
light on poetry—heavy on slam.
I learned the keys to success,
how to bring the audience into the fold,
the secret of winning that gold.

Never offer up a prayer as a poem,
mention God or admit to loving Jesus,
or the judges will nail you to a cross.

Never speak of love that isn't troubled,
incestuous or abusive.

Never recite a sonnet or any other formal form.
The rhyme, the meter, that poetic language
tend to confuse the judges. So alliteration
and personification are also out of the question
if you want to move beyond the first round.

I went to a poetry slam,
light on poetry—heavy on slam.

years later

a woman like you
is who I was searching for
a woman to be my sunshine
a woman tender enough
to be a cloud in my heaven
a woman whose heart
sings to me like a calm sea
beneath a denim sky

you took my breath away
that first day
that first look
that first word
and I still thirst for you
a woman
who I discovered
to be love personified

Water Falling Into Water

Seventy-five-dollars for a wine barrel
sliced in half by a band saw.
The cork hole now only a semicircle.
Oak staves still banded together
point skyward like the fingers
of cupped hands. Inside,
a crimson stain from the blood
of a thousand grapes.
I fill this circular casket with water,
a small pump and spray nozzle,
create a fountain
that will play that symphony
of water falling into water.
But, when I flip the switch
these waters bubble with chants
of migrant farm workers
from those picket lines of '65,
Huelga! Huelga! Huelga!*
Cesar Chavez asks for nonviolence.
The same nonviolence Martin preached.
That very same nonviolent
civil disobedience of Gandhi.
All I want is a fountain
that makes the music
of water falling into water.
But the past will not be quiet.
Yet, we do not listen
        —we do not learn.

* *Huelga* is Spanish for *strike.*

Fatherly Advice on Being a Poet

I've always wanted to be a poet. But, my father said:
Son, this is not a country that rewards poets.
Besides, all the famous ones are dead.
It seems a risky undertaking to me.
Be a milkman. Everyone drinks milk,
and all the famous milkmen I know are still alive.

Don't be a poet son. People won't understand.
No one will read your poetry; they'll all be watching TV.
And there will never be enough poets to form a union.
I'm a teamster you know. We meet in a big auditorium in L.A.,
thousands of union brothers and sisters.
We wear our union buttons,
cheer when they introduce our leaders,
cheer when they refer to management as the enemy,
cheer when they talk of wage hikes and strikes
if those management dogs don't come around.
Of course, we don't really have much of a say.
The union bosses run the show—we vote their way.

But son, poets meet in the basements of old restaurants,
the back rooms of libraries, in small coffee houses,
old musty yoga studios, or out-of-the-way art galleries.
You'll read a poem and someone will sigh,
then another guy will muse out loud,
"What the hell does that mean?"
You'll spend nights without sleep searching
for that perfect word, then hours rewriting.
You'll devote days to scribbling phrases on paper napkins,
the palm of your hand. You'll never be satisfied
with your latest poem. The next must be better, say more.
Don't do that to yourself son.
Be a milkman or a plumber or an engineer.
Join a union. Do something with your life.

But, as young men are inclined to do,
I ignored that fatherly advice.

Paris

is an intimate sidewalk café
on rue Paul Albert;
a perfect cup of espresso
with the woman who shares your bed;
old men who toss croissant crumbs
to pigeons in the park,
wink at all the young girls;
that crush of bodies
on the morning metro;
the young Frenchman
who gives up his seat for your lady;
being lost in the Latin Quarter
searching out
Hemmingway's old haunts;
tour boats that slip silent as light
down the River Seine;
that woman who gives you directions,
her English so superior to your French;
seeing the city from the top
of the Eiffel Tower;
lovers in the shadows
who don't care if you stare;
cobblestone streets
worn smooth by the footsteps of history.
And yes—those Paris nights,
reason enough to call it
the most romantic city in the world.
But in truth it's not the city,
it's the woman you're with.

Poetry Workshop

During the workshop
they talk of Plath,
Stafford and that woman
who lives up near Frisco.
They speak as if old friends,
on a first name basis,
these local poets
and those of notoriety.
They dissect stanzas,
even single words
in a struggle to understand,
then force meanings
of their own onto the page.
And I am certain
they have all missed the point
of poetry. It's a lot like being
with a woman. Enjoy
the moment—don't question it.

Shadow in the Garden

I couldn't see it then even with the words
               still wet on the Doctor's lips
Mother there, alive, breathing
          I couldn't believe
          I wouldn't
But now I have returned from where I watched
                    Mother cry
                    Father cry

          Today I see it
just beyond the open door standing in the shadow
face hidden by a black shroud
          But I turn away just as I did then
the words bring a hush to the room
Said in such matter-of-fact impersonal utterances
                 that reach out and take life

Father's Voice

I open my mouth.
My father's voice leaps out
with that mid-west inflection
even though I was born & raised
in Southern California.
He's here, somewhere
inside me, possibly lurking behind
my blue eyes—our blue eyes.
Those eyes closed one afternoon.
Then, that August night I listened
to him release his final breath.
I will never again hear
that fatherly pride in his voice
when he introduced me
to friends, *This is my boy.*

Shortcut to Heaven
—after the art of Barbara Ruys:
    Stairway to Heaven

I was lead to believe Heaven
is somewhere above the clouds,
maybe beyond the stratosphere.
I didn't realize you could get there
on a stairway less than five feet tall.
Does Saint Peter hang out on that
first landing, check your credentials
before allowing you to climb those
last four steps to meet God? And who
built this supernatural structural,
the same crew who crafted the Ark
for Noah? I'm not sure about that
multi-color scheme. The local
Home Owners Association may
have something to say about that.
And, do those spindly hand rails
meet city code? I can't swear to it,
but I don't believe the Bible mentions
a stairway to heaven being near the front
window in an art gallery in Escondido.
But, just in case
—what's their address again?

Baked Goods

I set my beach chair
at the foot of a small dune,
look south toward Ponto jetties,
late morning sun on my face.
The sea rumbles with its parade
of waves. A lone gull lurks
nearby hoping for a handout.
But all I can think about
is your mouth, the sweetness
of your lips and tongue
when I kissed you last night
in the kitchen, oven door
open, heat and the scent
of chocolate pouring into the room.
All I can think about is how
you tasted like homemade brownies.

For Those Women Who Don't Understand Their Man
read the fine print

Intended for personal use only:
Warranty is non-transferable, deemed null and void if unit is used commercially or stressed beyond the somewhat limited design parameters. Daily maintenance is required to ensure peak performance. Salsa and beer stains should be removed immediately.

Improper uses:
Doing dishes, washing windows and floors, scrubbing sinks and showers, vacuuming, doing laundry, cooking, pulling weeds, mowing lawns, painting or anything remotely related to household chores should be avoided at all times. Independent research has shown these activities to be detrimental to the delicate internal balance of macho and his feminine side resulting in a bad attitude, sulking and extended sessions of NFL live. Suggested remedies for these performance anomalies, should they arise, include: barbequed steak, carnitas burritos, Cajun style red snapper on sourdough, season Padres tickets, M&M peanut candy, spaghetti with spicy red pepper sauce, the promise of a big screen TV, any flavor ice cream, pickled jalapeno peppers and of course the dead sure fix of your appearance in a black peignoir.

Warranty work must be performed by an authorized dealer:
Any attempt to change, add or delete social graces, grooming habits or the general outlook on life will be met with resistance and resentment. The manufacturer offers their condolences on your choice and reminds you, there is a *no return, no refund* policy. Deal with it.

Lost & Alone

He shuffles past, little more than arms length away.
Dirty jeans, flannel shirt drape his gaunt frame.
A bedroll, wrapped in plastic, hangs from his shoulder.
He pauses, squints into the sun, turns, stares
right through me into the distance, his eyes
weary beyond their real years. His face, whiskered
& sun blistered. He continues his trek in a slow,
uneven gait, the scratch of sand on concrete under foot,
a man lost & alone in a city of three million.

Bicycles in the Park
Bush Park, Salem, Oregon 1993

Like gaily festooned ghosts
they roll silently
along narrow paths,
swooping, leaning,
one after another
at precisely the same point,
rhythm unbroken,
pedals hesitate,
helmeted heads
tilt ever so slightly.

A medley
of yellows, reds, blues
streaks across
the rich green of nature;
excites the eye,
embraces the heart
longing to ride,
to wear the shoes
that clip into pedals,
don jerseys with names, logos;
and bend the wind
around mirrored sunglasses.

Veteran's Hospital
Room 202

Old men rest,
pillows stacked behind heads,
eyes thick with slumber,
years heavy on their minds.
A morphine drip
the new cadence they march to.
They slip away, somewhere,
some other time.
Uttered fragments of thoughts
and questions.
The answers to be revealed
in their eulogies.

Flight

The sky is a Renoir,
maybe a Monet,
grays, subtle hues of blue.
The sea, a Van Gogh,
dabs of emerald and white,
texture of wind over ocean.
The horizon, unclear, unable
to separate sea and sky.
A scant formation of pelicans
drifts over in wingless flight
on a wave of west wind.
I recall a March evening
just before sunset, that glide
of pelicans past the window
as we exchanged wedding vows.
I don't believe in omens.
Yet, I know your love
lifts me in wingless flight.

The Wait

St Mary's hospital,
stark, angular, bold,
rises from a clutter
of medical buildings.

I trek a maze of corridors,
lefts, rights, elevators.
A final hallway leads me
to my mother's room.

There, a huddle of apparatus,
I.V. bags, a tangle of wires, tubes.

And that small figure
lost in a rumple of covers,
behind padded bed rails.

She smiles up at me.
Recognition,
but not a word.
I sit and wait.
After everything
she has done for me,
I can only sit and wait.

once again

it begins with a gray smudge of sky
& meaningless swells
mounting in the west
on a green blanket of ocean
& the mirrored flight of Pelicans
in silent revelry

With You

You open to me as a morning glory
obeys the rising sun. I know
how God must have felt the first time
He heard His name offered up in prayer.
And though I have become one of those old men
who, like my father, can't imagine where the years
have gone, I know where and with who
I want to spend those I have left.

Surfing *Grandview*

I hadn't expected much.
It seems to get in the way,
expecting, then not receiving.
But I had reason:
thick gray clouds smeared
the morning sky, the breath
of a distant storm swept
the ocean into a frenzy.

Yet, two cups of coffee later
sunlight fell from the sky,
the slightest suggestion
of whitecaps danced
on a now sparkling sea.

I hadn't expected much,
certainly not walls of green water
towering over dark troughs;
explosions of white,
violent and unforgiving;
fear and sweet satisfaction.

I am the Poet

I am the waves that eat the edges of earth,
I am applause awaiting life in the hands of an audience
I am the bomb, the mushroom cloud no one survives
I am that eternal flame on John F. Kennedy's grave,
I am the small tattoo that marks the target for radiation
I am the ancient streets where Jesus once walked
I am the clouds, the rain, hail and snow
I am the first soldier to die on Omaha Beach
I am Martin Luther King's dream
I am the sun, the moon and the stars
I am the shoe not needed by a soldier who lost a leg
I am the unwanted child murdered by abortion
I am the pimp, the priest, the felon, the altar boy,
      the gang banger, the soccer mom, the fireman,
      the Doctor, the drug dealer, the car salesman,
      the local bully, the prom queen, the meth addict,
      the alcoholic, the porn star, the postman, the illegal,
      the man next door, the ranch hand, the child molester,
      the banker, the musician, the store clerk.
I am the poet.

November Observation
surfer's lament

Morning sun on my face
Dismal clouds sweep in from the west
      warmth siphoned off
      by a harsh chill
      hiding in that brooding sky
Coffee still warm in my cup
I gaze across an endless reach of sea
      where meaningless swells
      roll off the horizon
Nothing suggests I abandon my coffee
      paddle out

Moments

I'm not going to tell you everything.
But I will say, I trust only that which
I have built with my own hands.
Take this poem. I trust it, even though
there is yet a single syllable
you would want to take from this room.
But, that is the way of poetry: mysterious,
with so many ways to structure a stanza,
fill those spaces between vowels,
and then there is the story waiting
to be revealed. Take our story:
built from the remnants of previous
heartaches; love salvaged like so much
scrap steel, valuable for its tonnage
of reusable emotions. But, as we
recycle our desires of decades past
we discover they no longer fit our bodies.
Yet, there are moments we collect,
like rare coins or the occasional
unbroken sea shell, that stitched
together, woven into our days
create these years of our love.

Café Encounter

There's a momentary lull in that un-intelligible murmur of café
conversations. And, almost as if on cue, she enters wearing
a fedora like men wore in the fifties and a pair of Levi's that fit
in a way Mr. Strauss never imagined. A raven-black waterfall spills
from beneath her hat, frames perfect features, tumbles down her
shoulders. Silver rings adorn several fingers, an uncountable number
of ornate bracelets hug her left wrist, huge hoop earrings dangle
against her neck. He can't help but wonder if there are other jewels
attached in more intimate places. Almost as if reading his thoughts
she looks his way, a suggestion of a smile on her lips. He notices
the black leather belt encircling her waist, its enormous silver buckle
like those given as trophies to rodeo stars. Immediately he conjures
up images of this woman atop a Brahma bull, dominating for the
required eight seconds before turning the animal loose to sulk in his
pen. Why isn't this woman wearing a diamond on her ring finger?
Is she the type who slips off her vows before leaving home, to tease,
make men wonder, fantasize? Or is she cold and hard, refusing to
give herself to anyone? He peeks over his morning paper, shifts into
surveillance mode. She catches him again, watching her. He should
know better, ignore her. This is what got him into trouble last time.

The Great Divide

You are the Rocky Mountains—The Great Divide.
Your peaks and ridges, your height and breadth
separate rivers and oceans, east from west.

Each time I see you draped across the continent,
bold and unyielding, is like the first time.
Your call invites me to hike canyons and rock slides,
scale majestic crags, steeples and ridges.

You seduce me with that white silence of snow fields
and glaciers, mountains assaulted by ice.

Your turbulent landscape tumbles through the continent:
Montana, Wyoming, Idaho, Colorado, New Mexico.
Yesterday, wooden wheels of the Conestoga crawled
through Medicine Bow and Laramie,
following the Sweetwater along the Oregon Trail.

Great rivers find their beginnings in your rills and creeks.
The Missouri, cascading cold and clear, swirls and rushes
to the Mississippi, the footprints of Lewis and Clark
lingering along her banks.

The Platte and the Arkansas roll across the plains,
mingle their waters with the Gulf and the Atlantic.

The Snake and the Columbia plunge toward the Pacific.
Once wild and strong, now strangled by concrete and steel,
valves and gates: The American Falls Dam,
the Lower Salmon, Brownlee, Grand Coulee,
Priest Rapids, McNary, John Day and Bonneville.
Monuments to man's battle with nature.

The Colorado gives of herself, is taken and used as she
struggles through the confines of Glen Canyon Dam,
Hoover and Davis, to complete her journey, to prevail.

Your valleys rich with the golden yellow and brilliant reds
of autumn aspen, the deep greens of spruce and pine.

You tantalize me with rock ledges jutting into cobalt skies,
snow covered glades, clumps of lodge pole pines standing thin
and straight, shadows crisp on fresh fallen snow.

Ghosts of the past sing in your canyons and across Two Medicine
Lake, where the Blackfeet live on land taken, then given as if a gift.
The songs of their brothers, Flathead, Shoshone, Cheyenne, Navajo
Nez Perce, Ute, echo down the slopes, lie buried in blood and time.

You are the Rocky Mountains. I will never know all of you.
I have seen marsh grass on Green River, dandelion
and strawberry leaves, red, green, brown, and the white
symmetry of an aspen grove in late September.

I have watched the mist across Lower Lake where Square Top
Mountain hides the morning sun; seen the rose crown with
its gentle purple cluster above vivid green, the alpine sunflower,
yellow petals bursting from a golden center, smiling on the valley.

I still hear the golden eagle's song in the clouds above
a small valley of blue stone, see the bighorn sheep
perched high on a crag watching with black eyes.

I have seen the mountain lion's beauty and deadly power;
the elk's majestic crown; antelope, coyotes and wild horses
where prairie schooners once stirred the dust of South Pass.

You are the birthplace, the haven, the final resting place:
your forests and steams and meadows, your rocky ledges
and snow fields, your bleak sage wastes and alkali flats,
your sand dunes and buttes and badlands.

You are the Rocky Mountains—The Great Divide.

Day Trip

We cruise Coast Highway.
The Pacific hammers away
at the bluffs on our left.
Off to the right, inland cities,
their mass of humanity,
heat and foul air.

But the California coast
is like a string of pearls:
beach towns too expensive
for our retirement checks;
too chic for your J Jill wardrobe,
my American made car.

At Last

She is the woman
I was born to be with.
Not perfect.
Yet, her flaws not nearly
as numerous as my own.
Her eyes, brighter
than that summer sun
I have always loved;
her mind, a thing of beauty.
But early in life
our paths detoured,
not to cross for seven decades.
She is the woman
I was born to be with.

Humpbacks

Out beyond the silver wash of sand
Below those blue green ripples of life
Gray shadows slip past unnoticed

Blind Boy Mending Fishing Nets
Manzanillo, Mexico

The face of the boy reveals little. But,
his vacant eyes, always fixed on the sea,
say more than most care to hear.

He is learning the secrets of the sea
from his grandfather and father,
yet does not go out in the family boat.

The boy threads a net with an old
wood shuttle, the way his father
and his father's father did before him.

He spends his days on the dock
listening to gulls cry, waves slap against
pilings. These sounds are all he sees.

On the dock a boy mends fishing nets
for his grandfather and father.
But, his dreams carry him out to sea.

The Wall

I step into our side yard, coffee cup in hand,
morning sun a few hours above the horizon.
The legion of flowers that divides our yard
from our neighbor's is chaotic with color:
reds that drive hummingbirds into a frenzy;
yellows that pop bright as a midday sun;
a sprinkle of orange and that blue,
or maybe it's purple, that mimics a sunset sky.
Then my gaze drifts to the neighbor's yard.
Not a blossom other than that huge crop
of dandelions, their white tufts ready to jettison
seeds that float, touchdown and establish
roots in hell, no respect for boundaries.
Also scattered about in a pattern as random
as the stars, tall, thick, grass-like weeds, stalks
beefy as Swartsennegger in his pre-governor days.

Only thing to do: keep them out, build a wall.
                              (a fool's plan)

Village Maiden

There was a woman—*but then,*
there always is—whose beauty
could not be masked
even by the darkest shadows
in those narrow village streets.

Her hair was the color of summer
wheat, the line of her neck
graceful as a gazelle and her
mouth said everything
without uttering a single word.

She wouldn't tell me her name,
didn't ask mine. Some things
are best left unsaid.

I lost count of our time together:
days in the garden where roses,
the color of evening's failing sun,
bloomed with reckless abandon;
nights in a room fresh from
a Van Gogh painting, our bodies
blanketed by starlight that fell
through naked window panes.

Then, I awoke to a note. Fearful
of her words I never opened it.
I couldn't accept a *Goodbye*,
couldn't make myself stay.

Now, any woman in the shadows
reminds me of that village,
that woman and her ice blue eyes
that constantly caught me by surprise.

San Francisco Sidewalk

A homeless man
slumps in a bus stop shelter.
Obscenities & pure nonsense
fall from his toothless mouth
onto the sidewalk. We step
over these unintelligible
explanations of his life.
Even after seeing
the Golden Gate Bridge,
Alcatraz & the Presidio,
it is impossible
to abandon this image,
leave it lying on the sidewalk.

Warning

I'm here to warn you.
Not about the health hazards of smoking
or those dire consequences
from too much booze and I'm not
even going to mention recreational drugs.
    You see this bloody wound on my arm?
Well, no you can't, but it's there,
beneath a bandage, trying to heal.
    The other day I pushed myself to the limit.
You remember the Siegfried and Roy incident.
Actually, it was more the Roy and a white tiger
incident. Well, that's got nothing to do with my arm.
I'm just saying, beware
no matter how familiar your surroundings.
    It's true, I was pushing the outer edges
of the envelope, like that San Diego photographer
who was eaten by a grizzly bear
a few years back. Thought he could
just walk up, snap a shot of her cubs.
That's got nothing to do with my arm either.
I'm just saying, don't take anything for granted.
    Yet, I continued to venture beyond
the parameters of my expertise,
much like my friend who went horseback
riding at a dude ranch in Montana.
Someone left a garden hose lying out
near the corral. His horse mistook it
for a snake, threw him, broke his neck.
Again, that's got nothing to do with my arm.
I'm just saying, things happen.
    Yes, I was caught up in a moment of machismo,
turned a deaf ear to my wife's warning:
If you're going to weed the flowerbed
be careful around the rose bushes.

Fairytales & Royalty

My thirty-something beauty, with your perfect
nose and chin, those perky new breasts,
you ask for all the things of fairytales. Yet,
I suspect your idea of a cottage in the woods
is most likely the Plaza Hotel in New York.
And the woods might be those potted plants
at curbside, coddled with the same care
given guests behind that chiseled stone façade;
or possibly Central Park, horse draw buggies
where lovers can hide from the world, reveal
everything to each other. Either way I feel
obligated to say, I may not be that knight
on a white horse for whom you search.
And, speaking of white horses, that's not my style.
I wouldn't be caught dead, even with a thirty-something
redhead, in a BMW or Mercedes. I drive a truck,
wear shorts and California shirts, spend hours
at the beach, sand in my hair, saltwater in my ears.
I have no desire for a woman who is willing
to *give it up* for a bank account and a flashy ride.
But since you asked, I do have a fantasy or two.
They have to do with a woman's neck, the small
of a her back and curve of her calf. But alas,
you are not a Princess, nor I a knight
in shining armor. But how close you came,
how very near to grabbing that brass ring,
for you see Miss thirty-something, I am a King.

Beach Talk
Overheard on Carlsbad Blvd

Two young women,
girls really,
push baby strollers
along the beach walk.
They march single file,
a small parade of youth.
Conversation is constant,
animated faces,
arm & hand gestures.
The girl in front,
tall, slender,
sun bleached hair
pulled tight in a ponytail,
a pair of oversize sunglasses,
a small tattoo
on her shoulder blade,
a fire breathing dragon
hugs her calf,
enough red ink to stop traffic.
And—there is that telltale
baby bump so hard to hide.
They pass my sidewalk bench.
She speaks to her friend
over her shoulder,
All I know is,
I'll never date a surfer again.

Terra Mar

I barely set foot on the sand when that pungent odor of rotting
seaweed engulfs me, sweeps me away like a rogue wave back
to my childhood where every day smelled of decaying kelp and
Coppertone sun tan lotion, the legacy of all who lived in a Southern
California beach town, those small communities clinging to PCH
like life itself depended on it, towns scattered along that ribbon of
asphalt like a string of pearls draped around the slender neck of the
Southern California coast, Manhattan, Redondo and Palos Verdes,
Belmont Shores, Huntington, San Clemente and Oceanside, Del
Mar, La Jolla and PB, where life taught you respect for the ocean,
her many moods, that sway of the moon, earth's rotation, whitecaps
born of a far-off storm, spindrift dancing in the sky, unseen currents
stirred by Neptune's scepter, and still you go down to the sea with
questions, expect to find answers in bits of broken shells, that
mystical glide of pelicans, a tangle of seaweed strewn on the sand,
and you listen to her voice late at night, at times angry with the
distant thunder of breakers, or nearly silent, so subdued you dress
and go down to the shore to quell your fears that somehow those
dark waters have evaporated into the shadowy night, spilled over the
horizon, yet, for those who love her, the sea is always there.

On the Make in the Museum

Last week his granddaughter's kindergarten class
swarmed the Getty like ants at a picnic lunch.
He was responsible for three of those invading
creatures so intent on becoming cultured
— or at least playing in the drinking fountain.
Ten minutes into the tour he saw her: a blond
with curves that rivaled any mountain road
he'd ever traveled. She smiled. He smiled.
They spoke under a Van Gough. Turned out
she lived just down the hill. He pointed
out a priceless piece to the children
as that blond and he headed for the exit.
This week is an outing to a local museum.
He's been asked to stay away. But why?
Certainly they can get crayon marks off that Renoir.

Eve

She claims the mineral waters
can cure anything, help me forget
the city, that other woman. So,
we drive along the Neskowin River,
up a snake-like road that flirts with
every bend of that torrent. The hot
springs bubble up at 103 degrees
in a large pool beneath a basalt ledge.
We find the springs empty, leave
our clothes on the bank, melt
into submission. In this Eden-like
garden I accept the apple.
A Jay cries from a nearby branch.

To the Sea

— for Jeff

beyond this barren stretch
of sand, beyond that chaos
of white water, out where waves
are born, your spirit still lives

we returned you to the sea
just as you asked old friend
the sea—the only place
you ever wanted to be

No Regrets

The college campus seems to sprout
from the lush green hillside.
Walkways web their way around
sacred halls of science and liberal arts.
Sidewalks are alive with small clusters
of students, like grapes on a vine.
You glance down at text books
scattered on the front seat of your car,
then at the surfboard poking its way
out of the back seat, nose resting
on the dash. You leave the parking lot,
head for Seal Beach, five miles
down Pacific Coast Highway.
Oil field pumps line the old road
like a flock of giant prehistoric birds
foraging for food, massive heads
bobbing up and down in a slow,
rhythmic pace that will continue
for decades, suck the earth dry.
The huddled houses of Seal Beach,
its ancient power plant belching steam,
come into view. You cross the San Gabriel
River, turn toward the ocean. You watch
the waves for a while, unload your board,
paddle out. This is to become the prevailing
scenario of your short lived college career.
Later in life, during a marital moment,
your now ex-wife throws those sporadic
college days at you, like a drunk tossing
darts at a barroom bulls eye. She complains,
You could have been anything you wanted to be.
I am, you say.

For the Kids

I went to a reading of local poets.
Now that's not unusual in itself,
it's just that they wanted a donation.
Actually they insisted on it.
Now I'm not cheap, but I questioned
with all the free readings I can attend
why pay and pretend I didn't have
something better to do with my twenty dollars.
It was a benefit for a private school.
You know, one of those places you send your kids
if you don't want them mugged in class.
And they do teach music and painting and poetry.
It was for the kids—so I dropped my money
into a big basket marked 'Donations' and wandered
in among the beret-clad intellectuals and art lovers.
Decidedly a different feel than Full Moon Poets,
where poets huddle together to fight off frostbite
and craft there lines around the Amtrak schedule.
This room had heat and a view, glass all around,
the Pacific only yards away. I stepped closer to take
a peek when a young woman approached. *Beautiful
isn't it,* she said. I turned and gazed at the remnants
of a classic California sunset. *Yes it is.*
She held out a big basket marked 'Donations'.
That'll be a dollar and a half. Now I don't
get to many of these charity events, and I'm not
sure of the protocol, but I was sure I'd have a drink
later, which in turn would necessitate a trip
to the men's room, so I asked if I could start a tab.
Now I'm here to tell you, I heard poets that night
that I had heard before for free and I can't remember
the last time I paid to pee. But hey—it was for the kids.

Day's End

A weak west wind,
unable to prod our wind-bell into song,
ruffles leaves of a Mandevilla,
its blood red blossoms alive
against a gray fabric of evening sky.
In the distance a train clatters by.
A lone Mockingbird sits atop a palm,
plagiarizes the song of a Pacific wren.
We listen to the thunder of waves
attack the bluff along Coast Highway.
The air cold, you wrap yourself
in a woolen cocoon of sweater.
I move closer on the porch bench.
Our shoulders touch, our hands
find each other. We sit in silence,
content with the symphony
of day's end—and each other.

Baptism

Morning rises, rumpled and gray,
like an old man from a restless sleep.
The constant concert of waves washes
the shore clean like God granting
absolution to the earth. This beach,
as close to heaven as I may ever get.

The years have tempered my desire
to be anointed in the roll and tumble
of white water, held up to the high priest
of accomplishment on each crest.

Yet, I cannot commit myself to the safety
of the sidewalk, alone, with only memories
to fill my hours. As a believer
I need the sun's warmth on my face,
that daily baptism in the Pacific.

Affair

Poetry never loved me, the way I wanted her.
We met quite by chance, but then
that's the way of the universe, unplanned
moments that become the rest of your life.

She was reluctant in the beginning. So,
I made promises I could not keep, spent money
as if I had it and took her home with me.

We spent seasons together. Winter evenings
her warmth cradled in my hands; spring,
she lay with me on the cool grass
of afternoon, but she never loved me.

Summer days our relationship burned
like a stretch of sand beyond tide's reach.
She taught me the language of the sea,
how to ask the sun for a crimson night sky.

Then, fall brought a brooding moon
and she held her words inside. Even
though she invited me in, to search
them out, taste their secrets, feel her
on my tongue, she never loved me.

So it was, year upon year, I gathered her in,
pressed the rest of the world from between us,
listened for the essence of her sighs
and realized, she may never love me.

Then, on a day when I believe I can
no longer call myself *Poet*, she comes
to me like the moon finds the night,
slow and easy. My muse surrenders,
gives herself completely
and I take her for my mistress.

Yet, this is not a sin against the world,
or the church, nor in God's eyes.
Merely an affair of consenting creativity
committed by anyone wed to poetry.

Tsunami
March 11, 2011

Japan quakes with an eight point nine.
And like a rock tossed into a pond,
tsunami waves ripple the sea.
On this side of the world we watch TV,
see a wall of water erase generations.
Killer waves muscle their way around
the globe. The death toll rises like a storm
tide. There is nothing we can do
but offer up a prayer. Life is not fair.
So I load my board, head for my favorite
surf spot, wait for some tsunami waves.

Tomorrow we mourn the dead.

A Weak Moment

There was lust in my heart,
like Jimmy Carter back in '76.
I needed materialistic
satisfaction. So I bought
a new truck with all those
extras and upgrades
I really had to have:
chrome running boards
like all the cowboy trucks,
huge trucker mud flaps
for all those slushy
California freeways,
a navigation system
to guide me through
these downtown streets
to find my way home,
electric door locks,
folding side mirrors,
tilting steering wheel,
Bluetooth so I don't miss
a single one of your calls,
reclining seats for that
snooze through the 5-805
merge and cruise control
for the open road,
even though I don't ever
want to leave town
now that I've met you.

Last Words

I can't remember the last words
I said to my father the day he died.
The stroke, so swift, knocked him
to the floor, into a state from which
he would never return. Was there
something I could have done
that would have made a difference?
Not unless I was Jesus, able to heal
the sick, raise the dead. Was there
something that needed to be said?
I should have told him I loved him,
that he was my hero, that I knew
of all the sacrifices he made. These
are things said about family after,
at the memorial, at graveside. But,
they should be expressed during life.
What were my last words to him?

Surf Check at *Old Man's*

I pull to the edge of the bluff,
switch off the ignition.
Merle Haggard is replaced
with the music of water
collapsing on itself,
waves birthed in far-off seas
by mystical elements of nature:
wind, fetch, bottom contours
and King Neptune's mood.
The morning air is uneasy
with a *Devil Wind*.
Spindrift peels from wave tops.
Today, giants roll in
twice the height of a tall man.
Double overhead is the proper
term. Fear and respect
is the proper approach.

Greener Days

A lone tree stands
on a bluff above the Pacific.
Bent from the constant caress
of an ocean breeze,
branches bare, stark
against an ever changing coastal sky,
not a single leaf or bud
with the promise of new life.
When I was a younger man
it was green with creation
and threw shade across
purple blossoms that crowded
the ground around it.
I would unfold my beach chair,
sit in its shadow, write poetry,
never a thought of that tree
becoming nothing more
than deadwood, or of me
growing into an old man
remembering greener days.

Final Word

Hear me, listen and I will speak
    So that deaf ears will hear, blind eyes will see
    Sickness will heal itself
    Gold will become the burden of the Poor
    Small children will understand, old men will stand straight
    Not one lamb will be lost and all things that are
    Will no longer be, but all that I have promised
    Will be given to those judged faithful and righteous.
    I will cast out those who feed on the soft underbelly
    Of the sheep entangled in the briars
    Giving call to the shepherd while foolishly tempting the wolf
    That strips the flesh and devours with ravenous gnashing
Hear me all of humanity
    You that rule with a powerful hand and little thought
    To the structure and order that has been given and received
    Only to be denied by your vile conspiracy
    Woven into the wanton neglect of children, the old, the sick
    The innocent animals led to the slaughter not as an offering
    But out of self-serving greed.
Heed my word now
    For I have spoken before with thunder from angry skies
    And lightning to pierce the darkest night
    Sending floods to ravage the land and destroy the mammals
    The birds and the fish that dwell there
    Man has failed his charge to rule the earth
    And succumbed to the Dark One
    Surrendering the place of honor
    Shunning the promise of eternity for pleasures of this world
    Self-serving excess that benefits no other
    That cast doubt on the righteousness and faith of mankind
Hear me now in this final word
    Death and the withering of flesh and bone, returning to dust
    To be scattered on the wind never to be gathered and reshaped
    Is the promise I make those un-faithful
    Whereas the glory of all things for all time
                belongs to the believer

On the Safe Side

My sister calls to say
they are in Hawaii, bought
a condo somewhere near a volcano,
can see steam rise from the earth
like an ancient tea kettle on the boil,
smell sulfur when the wind is just so.

I ask if she has ever heard the story
of Pompeii, or the fate of Spirit Lake,
how once the eruptions begin
molten lava, scalding ash follow?
She says it's perfectly safe, seldom
does the ground shake—much.

She invites me to visit, stay
in the extra bedroom, the one
with the view of the volcano.
I tell her I'll think about it,
say goodbye. *She must be insane,
a house at the foot of a volcano?*

I hurry to load my gear in the truck.
Running late. I promised my buddy
at the skydiving center I'd try out
his experimental parachute today.

Winter Afternoon

The one o'clock sun
warms me to the bone
after a late session
in cold January waves.
Out beyond the break
the sea boils with a frenzy
of feeding dolphins. Gulls
circle and swoop down,
join the feast while it lasts.
On the beach, a barefoot
woman walks at water's edge.
She wears a short leather dress
with a long fringe, a large
peace sign on the front.
I make a mental note of what I see.
There may be a poem here.

Coffeehouse

There are miss-matched chairs, small tables,
a couch against the far wall. A saxophone's
seductive melody sneaks in between muted
conversations. She is sitting across the small
room from him, her body draped on the couch.
Soft cushions reach up to surround her, embrace
that curve of her hips, gentle lines of her legs.
Radiant red hair cascades around her face
like strands of silk. She glances his way occasionally
in the course of conversation. A slight smile crosses
her lips when their eyes meet, or is it his imagination?
She is wearing a simple pullover sweater, light green
with a hint of yellow, the color of avocado meat
three days from ripe. The bulky knit reaches high,
encircles the delicate white flesh of her neck.
Her pants are a neutral color, something that might
be called bone or sand or maybe off-white by someone
ignorant in the terminology of fashion. She sits with her
legs crossed, the fabric of her pants pulled tight
against the curve of her thigh. One of her shoes lies
on the floor near the couch. A thin gold ankle bracelet
adorns her naked foot. He watches as she plays with strands
of her hair, then runs her fingertips over her temples,
closes her eyes. She gathers her hair between long
slender fingers, pulls it away from her face, leans back
into the plush cushions. Her beauty is fully exposed:
fine line of jaw, delicate ears with tiny silver earrings,
long arc of her neck. She breathes deeply. Her breasts
rise and fall beneath the green weave of her sweater.
A voice breaks into his thoughts, *Want another cup?*
He looks up into the inquisitive eyes of his girlfriend.
You look like you're someplace else, she says.

Sailor's Warning

beyond the early morning gray
fog lingers in slow retreat
of a rising summer day

a brush stroke of sky
whispers promises
paints the morning red

Waiting on Poetry

I cannot find those words
that often fall to the page,
each fresh in its own way,
never before said in that order.
Inspiration eludes me, my heart
still heavy with thoughts
of my father's death,
and this, my late mother's
birth month. Yet, I'll wait
it out, like the moon holds its glow
until stormy skies have cleared.
After all, the words are still there
like a child playing hide & seek.
I'll find them. And I know it will be
in the most unexpected places.

From the Start

If we had been in love
at the dawn of our adolescence,
would we survive those years
as high school sweethearts, you
wearing my ring around your neck,
me carrying your books between classes;
and all those semesters of college,
you the campus queen, me spending
too much time at the beach? Would
we have given ourselves to each other
then, the same way we do today,
if we had been in love right from the start?

When I'm gone...

I'll miss
that never ending march
of waves,
beach cobbles
and those blood red sunsets
that whisper promises
to the horizon.
I'll miss
the musical poetry
of our Soleri wind-bell
in an easy ocean breeze,
broken sea shells
and the glide of pelicans
above indifferent waters.
I'll miss
that smell of kelp
washed ashore
by last night's high tide,
warm sand beneath my feet
and those late moons
that linger in a morning sky.
I'll miss
the cry of gulls
scavenging on the beach,
those summer showers
that leave a rainbow behind
and I'll miss the hot summer sun.
But, when I'm gone,
and the memory of me
is scattered
along the California coast,
I'll miss you the most.

Barely There

— after the art of Monica Royal:
Barely There

I'd like to shed a little more
light on this not-so-subtle
suggestion of a woman,
delve deeper into the details.
There is not a curve out of place.
And that drape of fingers
over hip, the angle of her elbow,
that slight hint of neck
above the shadow that hides
her shoulder, falls across
her breast—mesmerizing.
Yet, considering the current
state of affairs, I'm not
going to say anything further
for fear of accusations being
bandied about, charges brought.
And, I didn't use my real name
as author of this poem.

Spoken Words

The problem with spoken words
is that they disappear into thin air
where we can never recover
that exact arrangement of letters
lined up this way and that.

And when we search our memory,
minutes and hours and days
cast a haze over the order of phrases,
inflections and intentions.

So here are my words to you
painted on the page, yours to keep
in a pocket or a drawer or between
the pages of your favorite book.

I love you.

Sylvia
Sylvia Plath 1932-1963

Sylvia, Sylvia, Sylvia—what were you thinking?
What happened that February morning?
You left bread and milk out for the children,
like a mother sending her young off to school.
And that note to your neighbor in the flat below.
Had you hoped he would somehow know,
come upstairs and stop you?
Sylvia, suicides have a special language
never understood by those left behind.
Did you really want to depart, end it right then?
What about the au pair? You must have known
she would soon be there.

Sylvia, Sylvia, Sylvia—what were you thinking?
Had you forgotten about your good omen:
that exact London flat, Fitzroy Road,
the same house where Yeats once lived?
Did you forget everything in your search
for a way out? Everything except
depression, the useless words of confession?

Was it spontaneous: the wet towels, the oven?
...the tent of unending cries.
(your metaphor, not mine.)
Or was it an attempt to heal the long festering
sore of your obscurity and Ted's fame?
Certainly he must shoulder some of the blame.
You know, he destroyed your last journals,
burned the words you wrote.
To protect the children, he said.
Sylvia, do you know you won the Pulitzer
two decades after your death?
And your words still take away our breath.

Sylvia, Sylvia, Sylvia—what were you thinking?

Ponto Jetties

A rusty bicycle leans against the railing
on Batiquitos Lagoon bridge. Nearby,
an old man tosses bread crumbs into the air.
Seagulls swarm in the cold morning sky,
scurry about stealing food from each other.
He speaks to them, calls several by name.
I can't tell one seagull from another.
He is a short man, wears a dirty sports jersey
with the number nineteen emblazoned across it.
A braid of gray hair dangles down his back.
Unruly tufts peek out from under his cap.
A matted mass of beard covers his face.
Bread crumbs gone, he bids farewell
to the gulls. Half-way across the bridge
he leans over the rail, shouts something,
then peddles off. I walk out on the bridge,
peer over the rail. Nothing but lagoon water
rushing out to sea with the receding tide.
What am I missing?
Is it something the seagulls said to him?

Gone

I awake to find her gone,
sheets still warm,
her slippers under the bed,
dog asleep in the corner.

I check the bathroom,
kitchen, my office
—nothing.

Not even a note.

The clock radio clicks on.
The Beatles.
All You Need Is Love.

A Note to My Editor

Poetry is too personal
to be judged by someone else.

How can you tell me
words I wrote
words from my past
words soaked in my own blood
words buried for years
      in fear and anger
words I gave birth to
words still warm from my heart

I think this should be…
or, *That isn't…*

How can you say that to me?

Vive la Différence

The French believe
it's the difference
that makes it worthwhile.

We've been to France,
climbed the Eiffel Tower,
Paris sprawled at our feet.

Here, that old power plant
stack soars into the afternoon,
Eiffel Tower-like only
in its phallic symbolism.

We spent nights in a Parisian
bed between sheets of desire,
stone bridges over the Seine
cold and quiet in the night.

Here, a beach town bedroom
masquerades as a Paris loft,
the Pacific, ancient as the Seine,
lies naked outside our window.

Love is different this time.
This time it's you and me.

Stormy Night

She lingers in a brooding sky
where wind tosses clouds about,

like a child's pillow fight,
in her reflected light.

Shadows thrown to the ground
hide among trees, their leaves

the color of new love.
I see her above. The same moon

that fell through my widow
that night we found each other.

Finding a Family Portrait

What can I tell you about it?
I found it one evening in an old envelope
along with dozens of dusty memories.
A photograph taken in Pat's living room,
the wall in the background covered
with pictures of The Beatles.
Father sat in a chair, me standing behind,
Pat to his left, Royan on his right:
patriarch, surrounded by family.
Mother had been gone for years by then.
Father said he talked with her every day.
What a shame her image, her love,
couldn't be captured on film that day
even though she was there.

Signal Hill Plane Crash
Southern California Military Academy, 1954

In my ten-year-old mind,
sneaking off campus
that January afternoon,
walking three miles
to Mike Bader's house
was a daring adventure.
What I hadn't counted on
was the plane crash.
I crossed Cherry Avenue,
walked up 20th
toward Raymond Street.
Overhead, a roar
like a hundred locomotives
in the sky, a streak of shadow,
a glint of sunlight off a wing.
An Air Force F-86 Sabre Jet
screamed past not more
than fifty feet above me.
I could see the pilot's face.
He looked right at me.
Seconds later the whine
of his engine morphed
into a thunderous explosion.
Seven people died.
I was the last person
he would see for eternity.

January Beach Walk

The sand beneath my feet
is damp with remnants
of high tide. The sky
is an apricot umbrella,
sun just over the horizon.
I reach out to take
your hand, interlock
our fingers so we
will never be apart.
But, there are only
my footprints in the sand
and this January air
is cold in my empty hand.
The gulls call your name,
or is that just me?

Seasons

Winter mornings
rush across the sea, a frenzy
of clouds stirred by winds
from the north, small shards
of gray sky seeping pale
prongs of sunlight that foster
hope, pointless promises.

Spring afternoons
blossom with the energy of fire,
glorious red skies weep tears
of jealousy over a cherry tree,
the common daisy, dandelions
pushing their way through a crack
in a downtown sidewalk.

Summer nights
slip from beneath that moon
balanced on the brink of sunset,
gild the horizon with waning
shadows, then quietly close
its arms around lovers waiting
for that sanctity of darkness.

Autumn days
ablaze with change, the earth's
foliage flinging off its dead,
colors of old blood and new
strewn along lonely paths,
swirling around those lazy
footfalls of strolling sweethearts.

Late in the Season

I park on the bluff along PCH,
tune in an *oldies* radio station;
watch the morning sea,
gray as those clouds
that cling to the bottom of the sky.
Only a hint of green in small swells
that stand up, then collapse on the sand.
In the distance, whale spouts.
Mother and calf.
The long arc of her back
glistens in early light.
It's late in the season
for returning whales.
On the radio, *Come Go With Me.*
The Dell Vikings from 1957.
I recall sock hops in the gymnasium,
a girl named Anita
and smoking Luckies
stolen from my dad's pack.
I notice the whales are gone now,
just like those sock hops
and that girl.
Late in the season, indeed.

Paris Days

There were days in Paris
when the River Seine
slipped quietly beneath
the bridge where we sat.

Those hours spent lost
in each other's eyes,
sweetest in that moment
like fruit eaten in the orchard.

Death of a Flower
Rose King 1921—2000

The room is dark, drapes drawn
against an Arizona afternoon.

We sit silently around a bed
where our beginning lies lost
beneath a rumpled blanket.

Everyone waits for the end,
or another beginning,
depending on your beliefs.

There is nothing left to say.
Father hasn't spoken in days,
sitting in a chair against the wall.

I step to the window,
part the drapes in search of
momentary escape.

Sunlight falls across the bed,
across Mother's face,
fills the room.

It reminds me of those who return
from near death experiences,
the bright light they speak of.

Mother stirs, sits upright
in spite of the Morphine.

My God, I'm still alive,
she says, and sinks back into bed.

Mother never speaks another word,
leaves us the next morning.

Day One

The sun mourns
your absence, sky
a drizzly gray.

The sea weeps
for that brilliant blue
of your eyes.

The wind silent
without your laugh.

I count the seconds
since I was last with you,
each minute a lifetime.

Train to Ipswich
Found poem from the Ryan's travel log

It's fairly simple you know, Hounslow to Ipswich.
Just buy two train tickets at Hounslow station.

The journey will take no longer than a few games of darts
and a pint or two at the local pub.

The Hounslow train goes to London Waterloo,
one of the big London main line stations.

Once you're there you must get onto the underground.
(watch your wallet and your wife)

Take it all the way to Stratford, the end of the line.
Then change to the Norwich train.

It will be coming from London Liverpool Street.
Or, take the underground to London Liverpool Street station,

where all the Norwich and Ipswich trains start.
It's a little complicated—but you *can* speak English!

The Loss of a Woman

I'm unsure of where to begin:
that first day I met her
or the last we spent together.
A Hollywood movie might
reveal our tragic ending
then flashback again & again,
like a rising & receding tide,
to tell the entire tale.
Lunch at the New York Deli
deserves a chapter all its own,
the way sunset is glorified
more than the proceeding hours.
Of course, she left one day.
The story wouldn't interest you
if she hadn't. But, I knew
that time was coming, maybe
even looked forward to it.
You see, as a poet, I thrive on loss.

Exposé

A good poet borrows;
a great one steals.

There were days when you bled words
like a wounded soldier seeps life. But,
more often than not the page starved,
hungry as a street woman who refuses
to trade back alley sex for a can of soup.

You spent your early years searching
for clear images; just the right verb;
wondered how you would turn a poem,
surprise the reader at the last instant.

You wandered dusty stacks in local
libraries, rooted out obscure poets,
lifted lines likes a child steals
cookies from the jar at Grandma's.

Then, throughout desperate decades,
those poets, and you, sent out poems
(bastard children that they were)
over mountains and waters where critics
ate your words like manna from heaven.

You received the Pulitzer in '65,
National Book Award in '74,
then, committed suicide by throwing
yourself off a bridge in Portland.
Poetry is a dangerous undertaking.

Now, people mourn your untimely death
unaware you had picked clean the bones
of many poets who went before you.

Express Line

Ten items or less. Cash only.
I stand here with a gallon of milk while an old woman
ahead of me places thirty two items on the counter.
Not a word from the clerk as he sweeps them
one after the other over the scanner. In a practiced,
robotic motion he tosses them, bouncing and tumbling
like dice on a crap table, toward the bagger.
Fifty three twelve, announces the clerk. The search begins
as the old woman rummages through a purse the size of New Jersey.
Oh dear, I know they're here somewhere, she mumbles,
spilling its contents clattering onto the counter: a comb
with several teeth missing, a large tortoise shell brush
entangled with a rat's nest of hair, three tubes of vermilion
lipstick, one without a cap, Oreo cookie crumbs stuck to it,
a plastic bag filled with cat chow and several unrecognizable objects
in different stages of decay. Finally, from the bowels of her steamer
trunk, she produces a fist full of coupons, slaps them down
like getting in a last minute bet on the third race. Of course the
orange juice doesn't match her coupon. The bagger is sent to make
an exchange. He never returns. *Fifty three twelve* says the clerk.
Another leisurely search soon yields a check book. *Oh dear, I seem
to be out of checks*, the old woman whines, and ventures
back into the abyss of her genuine imitation vinyl alligator skin bag,
only to emerge with a bank card. Seven swipes later, *Oh dear,
I can't remember my number,* she whispers. *Fifty three twelve*
demands the clerk. The old woman reaches into the ample cleavage
of her bosom, extracts a roll of twenties and concludes her business.
I slide my gallon of milk toward the clerk, *Have the bagger get me
another,* I say. *This one must be out of date by now.*

Summer Sun

this morning
a stormy ocean
reminds me of life
before you
I was never sure
when one storm ended
and the next began
but now
the sea of my life
is calm
the sky above dusted
with only a cloud
or two
and you my love
are the summer sun

Change

Just when you think you have them figured out
and you are ready to commit, they change
like an afternoon sky that surrenders those crisp white
cumulus to the disorganized pink and gray of sunset.
They are still alluring, sensual, still the same woman.
I remember Lynn Loomis in high school, how she
wore her hair in a long braid that fell down her back,
how it danced and swayed when she walked, how she
smiled at me in the hall on our way to U.S. History.
I was in love, high school love or maybe just lust.
Then she changed. She cut her hair. Pixie or bubble
or some such thing and began to hold hands
with Eddy Harris. The love affair was over, one-sided
as it was. Now, I'm with a woman unpredictable
as those sunset skies; the promise of love carried
on every breath of the evening breeze.

Sestina for Father
Clifton King Sr. 1917-2008

This would have been his 92nd year,
a celebration of all that makes a life:
his roots in a Kansas farm family,
the miles he walked to school each day,
riding the rails to nowhere, any train,
then the CCC and on to the service.

Nearly a decade passed in the service
of his country, the war lingered year
upon year, and the men he trained
as gunners fell, lost their lives
and he knew it would be, until the day
of surrender, that day his family

would welcome his return, and all families
could pretend to forget what their service
had done to these men, today, yesterday,
beyond the horror of those years.
It was a time of new beginnings, a new life,
a return to school, a new job, to train

for the future, or sadly for some, hop a train
to the past, leaving friends and family
to wonder about their values of life,
that dedication. Was it just lip service
like so many resolutions on New Year's,
trying to erase mistakes made every day?

But, my father rose above that, the day
he came home to California, a short train
ride where he had time to plan for the years
ahead, riches of this new world for his family,
a house in the suburbs, new dishes, a service
for eight for his new wife, for this new life.

Yet, it wasn't only the wealth of fresh life
he wished for, it was more like every day
filled with the joy you find in a church service,
that soul shattering sense of love a train
wreck couldn't loosen, that bond of family
members that lasts far beyond the years.

Yes, this is his 92nd year, and he spent every day
in the service of his beloved wife and family:
a long train ride from farm boy to giver of life.

Journey

I traveled this long road of life
searching for someone like you.
I never imagined the journey
would carry me deep into
my sixth decade, an old man
by any measure. I prayed you
would see beyond the sun
damaged skin, these wrinkles.
I searched for someone to hold,
someone to keep me warm
on those cold winter nights,
someone to laugh with,
cry with and make love with.
In you, my love, I found
the end of that journey,
the beginning of another.

First Moon

I peruse tide tables
like a priest scrutinizes scripture
searching out the secrets of life.

Yet, it's not all about the sea.
Just as God and Jesus are one,
so the moon's body is to the ocean.

And those disciples, sunrise
and sunset, create colors vivid
as the Pope's vestments.

Change is the message,
the way a full moon seduces
a dark, desolate sky.

Then that cold light, like a firefly
caught in an old mayonnaise jar,
often dies come morning.

But tonight's sky will be lit
with a sliver of waxing moon
just as on our first night together.

Chairs

The neighbor has a white plastic chair
sitting atop her trash can.
It reminds me of those chairs
my father had on his porch in Tucson:
hard, unforgiving, a blunt blade
of cheap plastic cutting into your back.
The neighbor's chair is unadorned,
plain white. My father's chairs
had Mexican beer logos emblazoned
on them: Tecate, Dos Equis, Corona.
You might say they were branded
the way ranchers brand their cattle
so they can prove ownership.
But we know rustlers don't care
and steal them anyway.
So it was a few years back
when Mother and Father wandered
Mexico in that old Dodge truck.
In need of chairs for those evenings
by the campfire and a couple extras
for the occasional guest,
they stopped at a small cantina
on the outskirts of a town, had lunch
and a beer on the patio, then
walked off with half a dozen chairs.
Years later, after my mother's death,
my father sold their place in Tucson,
moved to Nevada. But those chairs
remained on that porch. After all,
you know how risky it is to drive
a herd of stolen cattle across the state line.

Death

I was going to write a poem about death.
But, when I put pen to paper, nothing
came to mind. I'm not sure anyone
can write about it. After all, no one lives
through it. Well, maybe one guy. But he
trusted his disciples to write about it.
That's not really a firsthand account.

So, I've had to realign my thinking,
take a closer look at that pre-death
state known as life. I've survived
decades of that. Maybe we're here
to store up memories to take with us.

Final Journey

We shook hands. I said he looked good.
We both knew it wasn't true.
He said lately he's always tired, can't catch
his breath, gave up smoking last week.
In high school we smoked unfiltered
Camels, drank Bud from quart bottles,
never questioned the number of days in a lifetime.
I asked how long he was staying.
He said, *It all depends*. On what, he didn't say.
So I brewed some coffee and we spent the day
paging through the past: those school nights
we cruised burger joints in my dad's old Chevy,
motorcycle trips, all night beach fires,
killer hangovers, that summer we lived on eleventh
street in Seal Beach, those two girls, Leah and Mary,
the year we moved our families to Oregon, his divorce,
then mine, my mother's cancer, his brother's death,
his son's drug problem. We stayed up too late,
drank too much coffee, couldn't believe we'd made it
this far in life. Jerry left the next day. A week later
his daughter called, *Daddy died yesterday.*
I'm not ashamed to say, I cried that day. I called friends
to share the news. At least we had each other in our grief,
while Jerry journeyed on alone.

Tulip Fields in Holland
from a Magee Park Poets workshop

A Monet print hangs
on the far wall
of the reading room
in the public library.
Shards of sunlight slip
through the window.
A dance of shadows
from a eucalyptus
plays across the canvas.
The red and yellow
pigment tulips sway
in the changing light.
The windmill turns.
Water flows into the field.
Clouds drift through
a china blue sky.
We have ten minutes
to work on a poem.
I've forgotten the prompt,
wonder what to write about.

Whale Watching

I have come to our beach
to watch for whales.
Those steps down to the sea
are still here—all ninety four.
But high tides and angry surf
have washed away the sand,
leaving a carpet of cobbles
that glistens when wet,
lies in dry dullness
when baked by the sun.
Beyond the break, where the sea
is smooth with midday glass,
a whale spout. A wisp of mist
lingers in blue air, then disappears,
not a trace she was ever there.

Heaven's Lights

I walk to the edge of the earth
to watch a sunset. Yet the sun
simply fades from sight, cloistered
in clouds clinging to the horizon.

Daylight slips away
in an unceremonious play
of blue into gray into black.
Not a trace of crimson sky.

Now, a waning moon,
seemingly born of rooftops
and the leaves of a lone eucalyptus,
shimmers in evening's ebony air.

Being apart is like a failed sunset.
And, like the unselfish sun
that gifts the moon,
you are the light that gives me life

Tryst

We meet in the garden,
spend an afternoon in love.

This must be what it was like
those first days in Eden.

The weight of our bodies
sculpts early spring grass

that teases our flesh
like the flick of a tongue.

And when I kiss you
the sky bursts into flames.

Monet's Garden

The garden is raucous with red and yellow.
Bees and butterflies are overwhelmed with choices.
I find a bench in the shade, try to imagine
Monet resting here all those years ago.
Today, gravel pathways crunch beneath a crush of tourists.
A muted mix of Italian, French, that proper King's English,
and the American version, fills fragrance laden air.

Nearby, a woman talks on her cell phone in French.
Her words, music I don't understand.
In the distance, school children play, raise a bouquet of laughter.
A girl, voice so soft I barely hear her request,
asks that I take her picture.

I intended to write a poem, share this garden with you, the reader.
Perhaps even mention Monet's house and beloved lily pond
just beyond those green garden gates.
But, I see my lady coming down the path, sunlight in her hair.
She is the only poetry that interests me at the moment.
I will tell you about the garden later.

Royale Road Publishing